MW00946361

Breakfast with My King

Growing a Beautiful Love for Jesus through Morning Bible Study

Ebonee Rice

Breakfast with My King

Cover design by Devon Feldmeth
Editorial services by Camille Smith

ISBN-13: 978-1726040976
ISBN-10: 1726040976

Printed in the United States of America

Table of Contents

Acknowledgements

I dedicate this book to my nieces – the holders of my heart and pillars of my prayers. I am the woman I am because God saw fit to bless me with Earth angels who believe in me, challenge me and love me toward destiny. You are flowers. You are magnificence personified. You are my favorite part of the sunshine. Thank you for continuing to value my passion and for reminding me that God is real. I see Him alive in you all ways. I appreciate your beauty, fun-loving spirits and unique personalities.

Tonejah. Ashlee. TeJanna. Alicia. I'm proud of you, and I delight in how The Lord is leading and guiding your lives. I pray this study guide ignites a fire in you to continue living for Jesus, growing more intimately with Him and standing boldly for Him, even if you're standing alone. It's important. You're important. And God chose us for such a time as this.

I couldn't love you more. Thank you for loving me back. This is for you. So that you understand anything is possible with God. And that He, alone, called you. You are perfectly loved and adored by your Father. Please don't ever stop desiring to know Him more. It's worth it, I promise!

While I have your attention, sleepover this Christmas?

Introduction

I know you may not know me, but allow me to tell you about the time my life changed and the reason for why this study began...I'll make it brief.

In 2013, I moved across the country from Los Angeles, CA to Upper Marlboro, MD. Everything happened so quickly. Prior to moving, all the details fell so sweetly into place. I was excited to embark upon this new adventure. It did not take long after landing, however, for things to start unraveling. I began losing friends, money and most of all, patience. My new life was a series of unfortunate events, one right after another. I felt alone and it was hard. Nevertheless, I knew God was with me and that His goodness and mercy were within reach. I maintained a deep sense of knowing that only comes when your faith triumphs over your present circumstances.

Breakfast with My King began there – in that place and in that season. It was birthed out of a thirst for God's companionship. What started as a few Instagram posts, with associated #BreakfastWithMyKing and #BWMK hashtags, led to a community of people, spanning multiple time zones, who woke up to seek God with me. How special it has been!

I now reflect upon that season as a beautiful struggle. At the end of it all, I learned to be content in ALL circumstances, in times when I may only have little and in times when I have much. Most significantly, I learned that God's presence is paramount. There's nothing more important in our lives, no *thing* at all. Sometimes, being alone is the only way God gets us to understand that there's nothing for the believer outside of Him. In other words, for the *created*, there's nothing that we need apart from the *Creator*. In Him there is the fullness of joy, incomprehensible peace and strength for the journey. Yes, every good and perfect gift is there!

One reason intimacy with Jesus is a challenge for some of us to maintain is because we know that He sends us an invitation to be with Him daily. Over time we can develop a mentality that says, "If I miss time with Him today, tomorrow presents another opportunity." In concept, this is true. However, each day awakes its own occasion to learn and grow. There are mysteries He wants to share with you. There are problems He wants to solve through you. There are encouraging words in versus you did not read that are for someone you'll meet today. And there are seeds in your obedience that can only be cultivated through the Word. The bottom line is, intimacy with God is not just important, it is breath, life, hope, love, power, wisdom, enablement and nourishment. Without it, we die spiritually. This book is not written for those struggling to develop a Bible study routine, or for those who spend hours a day in their Word. It is a resource for anyone who wants to accept Jesus' invitation to breakfast (lunch or dinner). It is for the person who decides to be fed by Him on their couch, in bed, in the office, or during their commute to work.

Let's respond to Jesus' invitation. Let's meet Him at the table, hungry - not out of guilt or begrudge. But because He invited us. Each day, He's still inviting. Each moment, more enthusiastic than the last because He *wants* you to join Him. He chose to you to be with Him in the first place. He died for you to have access to your seat. And He know that His food is the divine empowerment for your life, health and strength. Let's answer today.

I'm sharing my Bible studies in hopes that it inspires you to grow closer to God. This devotional is organized to help you create your own notes with questions, thoughts and revelations. For the next 30 days and beyond, prayerfully, we'll spend mornings with our King, Jesus. The Bible declares in Psalm 119:147 ESV "I rise before dawn and cry for help; I *hope* in your words." God's Word is literally food for our souls and without it, we starve. Jesus said in Matthew 4:4 ESV "It is written, 'Man shall not live by bread alone, but by every word that comes from the mouth of God.'"

With this in mind, let's get started. It's breakfast time!

XOXO,

Eb

What is Breakfast with My King and how does this work?

BWMK is for the person, like me, who has been a believer but never developed a commitment to study the Bible. BWMK is for the beginner who has not attempted to follow a devotional. BWMK is for the avid Bible reader who wants to grow deeper in love with Jesus. BWMK is for anyone with insatiable curiosities and questions. BWMK is also for any nonbeliever who wants to learn more.

It's for you, your mother and father, your sister and brother, your neighbor, your small group, your friends, your daughter and your son. It's for all of us. Do you know that God **wants** to spend time with us? It's true! He delights in us as His beloved children. There's an intimacy that comes from learning Jesus' character, making Him priority in our lives, studying His Words and carefully housing them in our hearts. We are going to do more than read texts and passages from the Bible. We are going to study, meditate and slowly chew on God's words, and we're going to ask a lot of questions for context. That's the intention behind this book. It's about allowing what we read to transform us. We will walk away knowing that what we've read are more than mere stories. My hope is that we walk away from our devotion time with God feeling inspired, realizing these are historical, real life accounts of actual people and events.

This journey is about trusting the Holy Spirit to lead and guide us into understanding. Finally, it's about a commitment to building our lives and schedules around God's presence so that we can join Him in His work. We will accomplish this through daily time with God, studying His Word, Scripture memorization and prayer.

Although this is written as a 30-day study devotional, I recognize the diversity in my readership. Some of you may be Bible scholars and others may be learning about Jesus for the very first time. Each week has different content so if the Holy Spirit leads you to start in a certain chapter out of order, feel free to do so. Depending on how much time you allot to studying each day, you may either finish this book in 30 days or it may take longer. Go at your own pace, just don't stop. The only materials you need are a Bible and something to write with. I specifically do not insert the passages we're reading into the chapters because I believe it is important to spend time navigating the pages of the Bible. We will begin in the Old Testament with the Prophet Isaiah. The Old Testament can be divided into four sections, each providing specific focus on Christ. Isaiah is the first of the Major Prophets in the Old Testament. We'll then transition to Ruth, a historical book in the Bible meaning it recounts the lineage of Jesus. Be clear, the entire Bible is historically accurate. This book, specifically is considered a part of the historical texts in Scripture because it

11

details a period in history when Israel was ruled by God, not man. From there, we learn about the love of God and the love of Christians for one another in 1, 2 and 3 John in the New Testament. We will conclude this study in the Book of Psalms, found in the Old Testament. Here we will learn of God's forgiveness through the experiences of David via Psalms of praise and worship. The structure of the passages is not random. However, feel free to detour in Scripture as you are led.

I use the English Standard Version, but use whichever version you can. I also recommend worship music to set the atmosphere – every music platform has good suggestions if you do not already have a favorite. I have prepared playlists of songs for you to listen to each day, including some suggestions throughout this book. You can locate the Wake Up & Worship playlists on my Soundcloud at www.soundcloud.com/bwmk. You're welcome!

Here's what BWMK is NOT

1. A comprehensive guide on how to study the Bible
2. A rulebook on what you must read every day
3. A mundane, ritualistic checklist that ensures your Christianity

Remember when spending time with someone you love, like God, it's never the same. Don't make time with God boring!

Before we begin

My people are destroyed for lack of knowledge; because you have rejected knowledge, I reject you from being a priest to me. And since you have forgotten the law of your God, I also will forget your children – Hosea 4:6. If you're reading this and wondering who this Jesus is that I profess, keep reading. You don't have to be a Christian to study through this book, but it will not make sense to you if you do not invite Jesus into your heart. I'm going to give you the opportunity to know Him right now. No pomp and circumstance – just you and Him. Ask Him to show Himself to you. Invite Him into your life. Tell Him there's a hole in your heart only He can fill, and you want to **know** that He is real. Take your time here – I'll give you a minute.

If you've prayed this prayer from your heart, you are now saved meaning rescued from Hell and eternal damnation. Through the next few weeks, you and Jesus will journey together on an adventure that will allow you to truly get to know Him. It won't be easy, but I'm excited for you! I pray that you get in a Bible-believing church and surround yourself with people who will help you walk with Christ. He'll do the rest to ensure that every soul who seeks Him finds Him. We call that "Amazing Grace."

Before we read, we need revelation. Put this book down and ask the Holy Spirit to give you revelation over the coming days and weeks as you read and study His Word. Ask Him to guide you and to reveal Himself to you. Let's pray.

Holy Spirit, come into our lives. We are open and ready to receive all that You have for us in Your Word. Show us, Teacher. According to James 1:5-6 "If any of you lacks wisdom, let him ask God, who gives generously to all without reproach, and it will be given him." Give us wisdom, God. Reveal Yourself to us in ways we never imagined. Open the eyes of our understanding so that we can truly know You. Speak to us through Your Word. Allow us to understand, to hear and to apply the truths of the Scriptures. Now, Lord, we repent for any ways we may have ignored Your calling to be with You. Forgive us and let us be sensitive to Your desire to spend time with us to teach, love and empower us. Give us a fire for your Word, and a hunger and thirst for righteousness. Thank you, Holy Spirit. I pray this is Jesus' name, Amen.

Week 1: Getting started

Song suggestion: "Come Out of Hiding," by Steffany Gretzinger

Good morning!

I trust you are well, resting in the arms of the One who pursues, loves and adores you. As I type this, tears are streaming down my face. I'm listening to one of my favorite Gospel artists and while worshipping I heard the Holy Spirit say "this isn't about you." Truthfully I feel so inadequate, and completely unworthy to do the Lord's work. Conviction fills my heart and my insecurities melt into gratitude. I know that God uses, loves and empowers us so that even the least can bring Him glory.

I'm excited to study the Bible with you. I'm excited about what God is going to reveal to us through His living, breathing and life-giving Word. I'm also thrilled about how we're going to change for the better. If you're like me, you may have made some decisions to live differently, act righteously and hold yourself to a higher standard. I believe God deserves our best selves and that this world is broken and dark without Jesus. We must be the light to let others know that there is hope. Jesus lives, reigns and saves. His Holy Spirit gives us permission and authority to change the world.

I don't know about you, but I want to get to that intimate, holy, and sacred place with God where He reveals mysteries to me. That place where He answers life's difficult questions. I am more passionate than ever. I have more questions than ever. I have more enthusiasm than ever. Are you eager to share in intimacy with God? Let's move forward on the path toward perfection in the image of God's Son, Jesus, whom He forsake for us. Let's work on becoming better every day through the transformative power of God's Word. Let's welcome questions and revelation as we endeavor to journey toward understanding.

I once heard a quote that goes, "We're all just walking one another home to Heaven." Isn't that beautiful? I'm honored that you decided to travel with me through the Scriptures. Ready to eat? Let's start in Isaiah.

Things to know about Isaiah – we'll be studying Him all week so put a bookmark in this page to refer back to.

1. The name "Isaiah" means "Jehovah saves" in Hebrew. That's why we're starting in Isaiah – salvation is the root of the Christian faith.
2. Little is known about the Prophet Isaiah, except that he was the son of Amoz.
3. The book spans from around 740 to 680 B.C., which is from the time Assyria destroyed the Northern Kingdom of Judah

(Israel) during the reigns of Ahaz and Hezekiah all the way through Babylonian captivity.

4. The main theme of the book is the message of salvation (which means God sent His Son, Jesus, to die in the place of mankind in order to allow us access to Heaven and forgiveness for our sinful nature – see John 3:16 for more on this).

5. Isaiah is written in two parts:

   a. The first half of the book is Judah in the days of the Assyrians.

   b. The setting of the second half of the book is Babylon, then Jerusalem again, and then beyond.

6. Isaiah's words were primarily directed to the nation of Judah and the people of Jerusalem.

7. The Book of Isaiah is a part of what's called The Prophetic Books being that he was a prophet, and the book is surrounded by other prophetic books in the Old Testament. Look up "major" and "minor" prophets of the Bible for more context on this.

Day 1

Praying for the world

Waking up to Breakfast with God

"I rise before dawn and cry for help; I hope in your words." Psalm 119:147. Greet Him this morning!

This is a heading that is repeated every day. Commit to waking up each morning with a personal greeting of thankfulness and surrender. I encourage you to either repeat the greeting below or create your own. Starting this way will help you establish a relationship with God and acknowledge His majesty. Remember, you're not just meeting with someone regular. While Jesus is our friend, He's also King. Direct everything in your life around making Him King of all.

> *Good morning, God. Good morning, Jesus. Good morning, Holy Spirit. I'm so thankful for another day I get to worship you with my life. Right now I give You my hands to be used to build Your kingdom and Church. I give You my feet that they will follow wherever You lead. I give You my heart that it may feel what You want it to feel, and that You would replace my desires with Your desires for me. I give You my mind that You may clothe it with*

excellent, pure and holy thoughts. I cast down any thought that tries to exalt itself against the knowledge of Christ, in the name of Jesus. I give You my mouth that You may speak through me, that I may speak life, and that I may speak the truth with love and power. I give You my eyes that I may see others the way You see them. I give You my ears that I may hear, discern and be empowered to obey Your voice. I give You my will. I surrender my life to You and die to my flesh right now. I'm expecting miraculous and wonderful things today....all for Your glory. I just want to make You smile. I love You forever!

Passage

Isaiah 1:1-20

Study notes

1. Write your initial thoughts on this chapter. How is the Holy Spirit speaking to you? If you've never heard from the Holy Spirit ask Him into your heart, then ask Him to help you understand what you're reading.

2. I had to read this a few times because there's so much here and I didn't want to miss it. Below are my notes about what

stood out to me. Jot down (or think about) what stood out to you. Why do you think those verses caught your attention?

   a. I love headings. Whenever I see them I try to pay attention because they really set the tone for what I'm about to read. In my ESV (English Standard Version) Bible, it reads "The Wickedness of Judah." Naturally, my first thought was "DANG! What did Judah do?!"

   b. Likewise when a verse starts out with a command like "Hear," I focus on what the messenger was trying to get folks to listen to. And who the folks are that should be doing the listening. Context is important!

   c. Verse 5 pierced my soul. Whenever the Bible talks about the heart, I do a heart check. I skim my own heart space for ungodly patterns. Take a moment to examine your heart by asking God to show it to you.

3. Verses 1-3 made me cringe. When The Lord gives an analogy, sometimes it's a tough pill to swallow. A donkey though, God? Sheesh! What did they do to deserve this type of harsh lip from God? Keep reading.

4. Verse 4 lists the charges God is bringing against them. I thought "despise" was such a tough word. Again, I'm thinking what did the Judeans do in order for The Lord to speak to them, through Isaiah, like this?

5. Let me pause here. I feel the need to distinguish between Judah and Jerusalem, mainly because I forgot my old Bible

study lessons on this subject and needed clarity as I read about the people in Isaiah. Hopefully this clears it up: Israelites had a single kingdom during the reigns of Solomon and David. After the death of Solomon, the country was divided into two independent kingdoms. The southern region came to be called Judah, which consisted of the tribes of Benjamin and Judah. Jerusalem was their capital. The northern region was called Israel, which comprised the remaining ten tribes. Samaria was their capital.

6. Okay, so verse 8 - Who is the daughter of Zion? It means an ideal city personified.

7. In verse 9, what survivors is Isaiah talking about? What did they survive? Their land had been attacked and occupied by their enemies. Isaiah is speaking to those who remained.

8. Verse 11 reminds me of 1 Samuel 15:22, "And Samuel said, "Has the LORD as great delight in burnt offerings and sacrifices, as in obeying the voice of the LORD? Behold, to obey is better than sacrifice, and to listen than the fat of rams." I love it when Scripture parallels like this. See if you find any other examples of this in today's passage.

9. When Isaiah said, "Bring no more vain offerings," I thought of how many times I've presented a vain offering to God. I thought about how many times I've done things for my own glory whether on social media or in real life.

10. Parallel verse 11 to Numbers 28:11 and 1 Chronicles 23:31. Read them and break down the similarities.

11. Verses 14 and 15 describe how God denounced the people's worship practices that were originally meant to bring Him glory. Isaiah tells them how they have defiled worship by using it to manipulate God. They mixed in elements of Canaanite religions where they worshipped many gods, and used worship as a means to escape its original purpose. Have you ever manipulated God? I have. Take a moment to repent (which means to ask for forgiveness with the intention of never doing it again).

12. God then says, through Isaiah, what the people are charged with and the consequences of their actions. While doing this, He explains how to get back right with God. What a good Father.

Prayer focus

In the coming days, you will lead daily prayer. I'll kick us off this morning.

Dear Lord,

Thank You for Your Word. I pray for fresh revelation today. I ask that the Holy Spirit breathe on His Word and teach me His ways. Show me the mysteries of Your Word. Make it clear to me. I pray for the state of the world. I pray that I be one who stands as a beacon of light and pillar of truth for my generation. I pray for the leaders of governments, and all those in positions of power and influence. Please bless them to make Godly decisions with Godly wisdom. Raise up leaders that don't bend in the face of hardship or persecution. I pray that you remind us about your judgement and power. Don't let our hearts be hardened toward You, Lord. I want to delight in Your Word. I pray that it flows from my heart and overtakes me. I'm looking forward to the knowledge and perspective I'll gain over the course of this book. Thank You in advance for Your continued work in me. In Jesus' name, Amen.

Weekly memory verse

Stop regarding man in whose nostrils is breath, for of what account is he? Isaiah 2:22 (ESV)

Notes

Day 2

Social justice and the courage and compassion to do our part

Waking up to Breakfast with God

Greet Him this morning (Psalm 119:147 tells us why)!

Passage

Isaiah 1:21-31

Study notes

1. Write your initial thoughts on this chapter. Can you see yourself anywhere?

2. Again with the headings. The heading for the second section of Chapter one says "The Unfaithful City." Already I have some questions:

    a. Who was unfaithful?

    b. Who were they unfaithful to?

    c. In what way(s) were they unfaithful?

    d. How, if at all, did they reconcile their unfaithfulness?

    e. What were the consequences of their unfaithfulness?

    f. How do I see myself in this story? We've all been unfaithful before.

3. When Isaiah uses the word "whore" to describe the city/people of Jerusalem/Judah, what he is saying is that their

covenant with God is comparable to a marriage. When they turned their back on God by worshipping other gods and manipulating their worship, they cheated on Him and departed from their covenant with Him. What is God saying here?

4. It's so interesting to read verses 22 and 23, which remind me of how much God loves justice. When I launched my website, Ebonee Speaks, I decided to focus on the intersection between Jesus and justice. Jesus talks a lot about the poor, disenfranchised, and refugees of the world. In these verses, I see how God uses Isaiah to tell of their abuses. What can we be doing to advance God's desire for a just and fair society? Think about it. The world needs us to do our part.

5. God calls the Judeans, His people, His enemies in verse 24. Remember they were originally God's people whom He was in covenant (marriage) with. Why does He do this?

6. Reading through verse 26, Isaiah is warning them that God will get rid of the wicked. He will separate them and only leave those who have not rebelled against Him. Aren't you glad that God destroyed our rebellion? Aren't you glad that Jesus is the answer for our mess and shame? Reading this is was so emotional for me. Let's pause here and thank God for His Word that convicts, critiques and corrects us.

7. The word "justice" appears again in verse 27. Whenever we see words or themes repeated in Scripture it means it's important and we should pay attention to seek understanding.

8. When Isaiah talks about "oaks" and "gardens" in verses 28 and 29 what do you think he means? It's likely (via my Crossway ESV Study Bible) that he's referring to some type of Canaanite, pagan rituals that the Judeans should be ashamed of practicing.

9. God ends this chapter by saying that they will self-destruct and burn without repentance. Y'all, I had to stop and repent right here. This is such a convicting passage. I'm thankful God gives instructions, through Isaiah, on how to get back right with Him. Is there anything you need to repent of?

Prayer focus

That God gives us a vision of social justice. Pray that we have enough courage and compassion to do our part.

Weekly memory verse

Stop regarding man in whose nostrils is breath, for of what account is he? Isaiah 2:22 (ESV)

Notes

Day 3

Walking in the Light of the Lord

Waking up to Breakfast with God

Greet Him this morning (Psalm 119:147 tells us why)!

Passage

Isaiah 2:1-5

Study notes

1. Write your initial reactions to the chapter. How is the Holy Spirit speaking to you?

2. My title says "The Mountain of the Lord." My initial thought was "I'm ready to learn about this mountain!"

3. Verse 1 says "The word that Isaiah the son of Amoz saw concerning Judah and Jerusalem." A couple things:

   a. Judah is the people.

   b. Jerusalem is the place (capital).

   c. Judah was the fourth (of twelve) sons of Jacob, and the first to go into battle in the Book of Judges against the Benjamanites (people from the Tribe of Benjamin. The name means "praise" or "thanksgiving" in Hebrew. David and Jesus are both descendants of the Tribe of Judah, which means all the people born from him and his children through generations. How cool is it that Jesus is born through the lineage of "praise" and "thanksgiving." How much cooler is it that "praise" and "thanksgiving" is first before any battle? I love the Bible!

    d. Am I missing anything about this verse?

4. Doesn't this chapter open so reassuringly?!

5. I had some questions about verse 3 when I read "the God of Jacob?" Why is Jacob always specified? Isn't God the God of everyone? Why does Jacob always get the shout out? Here's what I learned:

    a. Jacob is the third descendant with whom God made a covenant (remember what that means?).

    b. He is the son of Isaac and Rebecca, grandson of Abraham and Sarah, and the younger twin brother of Esau.

    c. He is the father of the 12 tribes of Israel.

    d. His name is later changed by God. To what? Why?

6. When is the "latter days" Isaiah refers to in verse 2? It's an expression for the future beyond the horizon. Some people think it refers to the time of Jesus, but it isn't clear if that's what Isaiah means. What is clear is that he's talking about a time in the future.

7. Verse 3 talks about Zion. Zion is used as a name for the city of Jerusalem, the land of Judah, and the people of Israel as a

whole. As the Bible progresses, the word "Zion" transitions from referring primarily to a physical city to having a more spiritual meaning.

8. This is such a passage of hope. Isaiah predicts, through his visions by God, that the people will live "in the light of The LORD".

   a. Real quick! LORD or Lord in the Old Testament is used in place of Yahweh or YHWH to follow the tradition of the Israelites not pronouncing or spelling out God's name because it's too sacred. YHWH is Hebrew for "I Was," "I Am," "I Will Be," and because certain vowels are missing in the Hebrew language the vowel sounds/letters are uncertain. It's commonly pronounced how it's spelled here, "Yahweh."

9. Though Isaiah's predictions about the timeframe are unclear (it's likely he's referring to the coming of the Messiah, but not certain), he predicts a hopefulness in the life of Israel.

Prayer focus

That we will "walk in the light of The LORD."

Weekly memory verse

Stop regarding man in whose nostrils is breath, for of what account is he? Isaiah 2:22 (ESV)

Notes

Day 4

The pride of man and our desperate need for a Savior

Waking up to Breakfast with God

Greet Him this morning (Psalm 119:147 tells us why)!

Passage

Isaiah 2:6-22

Study notes

1. Write your initial reactions to the chapter. How is the Holy Spirit speaking to you?

2. "The Day of the LORD" is my heading. Here Isaiah is transitioning from feelings of hopefulness among the Judeans to feelings of guilt. Why? In contrast with the "latter days," God rejects the people during Isaiah's time for their greed, pride, oppression and idolatry (putting other gods before the true God).

3. I can't get over verse 8 which reads, "they bow down to the work of their hands." Why in the world would you worship something you created with your hands? We do it all the time. Think: material things, status, money, ego, etc. Can you think of a time when you've done this? If so, repent.

4. "Do not forgive them", from verse 9, signifies how Isaiah has given up on his generation. He's tattling on the people who've rejected God. In fact, he doesn't even want God speaking to them.

5. There is a huge emphasis, in these verses, on how God feels about human pride (see 12-19). If you are not actively combating pride, it's crept in. Why do you think that is?

6. Do you notice any themes being repeated in verses 12-21? If so, what are they?

7. Verse 22 is my favorite! I literally wrote in my Bible "Stop tripping off humans!" Isaiah is speaking to the weakness of human power and pride.

Prayer focus

Pray against the pride of man and for our realization of our desperate need for a Savior. Repent of pride if you have not, according to Proverbs 8:13.

Weekly memory verse

Stop regarding man in whose nostrils is breath, for of what account is he? Isaiah 2:22 (ESV)

Notes

Day 5

Praying for government, and the leaders of the world

Waking up to Breakfast with God

Greet Him this morning (Psalm 119:147 tells us why)!

Passage

Isaiah 3-4:1

Study notes

1. Write your initial reactions to the chapter.

2. "Judgment of Judah and Jerusalem." My initial thoughts: Uh-Oh!

3. Verses 1-15 are bookended with "the Lord God of hosts." These verses describe God's intention to deprive Jerusalem, and the people of Judah, of a human leader in their time of crisis. God is taking away so much from these people. Can you list all the things God promises to take away from the Judeans for their rebellion, according to the Prophet Isaiah?

4. This profile of Judah "under judgment" can be broken into categories for verses 1-15:

    a. Verses 1-7: shortages of food, water and competent leaders

    b. Verses 8-12: why Judah is ripe for judgment

    c. Verses 13-15: God's evidence against Judah

5. What I love is that even as God is speaking about judgment, He always looks out for the righteous (verse 10).

6. Wait. So notice the transition in verse 16 when Isaiah says, "daughters of Zion." I'm wondering why he singled out the ladies.

    a. For emphasis, Isaiah in verses 18-23, describes what the women wear and how they proudly adorn themselves. Unfortunately, this is what they devoted much of their lives to.

    b. God says, through Isaiah, that they will be humiliated for their pride and desire to use lust to lure men (verses 16-17).

    c. Why doesn't Isaiah mention the men? I don't know. It could be the context of the time; however, the list of extravagant female wardrobe accessories (in verses 18-23) matches the list of male leaders God is taking away (in verses 2-3).

    d. Do you feel more compelled to honor God with what you have or to adorn yourself with more and neglect Him? Please don't think this verse means that God doesn't want us to have nice things. That's a shallow attempt at the text. Verse 16 clearly states the condition of the women's hearts. Realize how quickly God can take it all away.

7. In verse 25, Isaiah predicts the defeat of the men of Judah.

8. In verse 26, Isaiah predicts the defeat of the women of Judah.

9. It's interesting that Chapter 4 has one verse that continues from Chapter 3. Verse 1 says, "Seven women shall take hold of one man." Woosh! In exchange for removal of their shame, the daughters of Zion will have few men to choose from as husbands..."only let us be called by your name." The eligible bachelor game among the Judeans is sparse. This reminds me of...well...I digress.

Prayer focus

Pray for government and the leaders of the world.

Weekly memory verse

Stop regarding man in whose nostrils is breath, for of what account is he? Isaiah 2:22 (ESV)

Notes

Day 6

Godly revelation

Waking up to Breakfast with God

Greet Him this morning (Psalm 119:147 tells us why)!

Passage

Spend time in His presence. We have read A LOT of information. Review Isaiah 1-3, 4:1.

Study Notes

1. Did anything new stick out to you?
2. What can you take away to apply to your life today?
3. What's one commitment, based on the passage, you can make right now?
4. What are you meditating on?

Prayer focus

Pray for revelation while reading. I encourage you to write down your thoughts/prayers and review them later.

Weekly memory verse

Stop regarding man in whose nostrils is breath, for of what account is he? Isaiah 2:22 (ESV)

Notes

Day 7

Spending personal time with Jesus

Waking up to Breakfast with God

Greet Him this morning (Psalm 119:147 tells us why)!

Study notes

- Spend time in His presence.

- Write freely and have a discussion with Jesus. LISTEN for His voice as you write.

- Turn on worship music -- sometimes I even dance and sing (off key) with Jesus. Song suggestion: "All" by KJ Scriven.

- Reflect/Evaluate your own life in the context of what you read this week.

- Have fun!

Applying God's Word

How does any/all of this apply to you? Jot it down.

Weekly memory verse

Stop regarding man in whose nostrils is breath, for of what account is he? Isaiah 2:22 (ESV)

Notes

Week 2: When God interrupts your life

Song suggestion: "Known" by Tauren Wells

Good morning!

How was reading through Isaiah? I know it's a lot of information but the important part is that you're waking up each day with an expectation that Jesus is joining you for breakfast, and He is. This week we're switching gears to the Book of Ruth. Why? Firstly, I love the book and it's short. We're going to read the entire thing. Secondly, it's an incredibly important piece of history. It's a beautiful love story that is deeply rooted in relations and culminates in each of our redemption stories. You'll see what I mean. Get ready to learn. I hope you enjoy it as much as I do! Even if you've read Ruth 100 times, there's more to uncover.

On a personal note, I've been listening to the song "Oceans" by Hillsong on repeat for days. DAYS! It perfectly describes the season of life I'm in right now. I cannot even begin to tell you what the future holds, but I am asking God to give me faith that doesn't mind living without borders, limits nor hesitation. I desire a life of hope and fullness, completely and fully dependent on God who I believe has "plans to prosper and not to harm me" (Jeremiah 29:11). My favorite part of "Oceans" says, "Spirit lead me where my trust is without borders. Let me walk upon the waters wherever you would call me. Take me deeper than my feet could ever wander. And my faith would be made stronger in the presence of my Savior." That is my prayer, and I'm hoping that you would ask for this type of faith as well. It is the type of faith that walks, carries and sustains, it doesn't play small for anyone or anything, and it trusts God to write the story of our lives with the end reading "Well done,". This week, as we meet God for breakfast, let's exercise our faith over everything else. If you find yourself unable to have faith in certain situations, you know where to run: to the never-ending well! And with that, let's eat.

Things to know about Ruth – we'll be studying this book all week so put a bookmark in this page to refer back to.

1. Ruth is a Hebrew name that means companion, friend, vision of beauty.

2. The Book of Ruth is set about 50 to 100 years before the birth of David. She is his great grandmother. This is important because Jesus is in the lineage of David. You'll want to pay attention to how Ruth becomes a part of the bloodline of David, and therefore of Jesus. She's literally redeemed into His family. That's a perfect illustration of our relationship with Jesus. When we accept Him in our hearts and believe He is the Son of God, we are saved and redeemed into His family by spiritual adoption. How cool!

3. The Book is set during a time of great trouble in Israel due to many disobeying God.

4. Despite the Israelites' disobedience, the story of Ruth gives us a picture of how God can guide us through difficult times.

5. God blessed Ruth because she committed her life to helping others.

Day 8

His redemption through Christ

Waking up to Breakfast with God

Greet Him this morning (Psalm 119:147 tells us why)!

Passage

Ruth 1

Study notes

1. Write your initial thoughts on chapter 1. How is the Holy Spirit speaking to you?

2. The first chapter is a brief introduction where we see that Naomi has lost both her husband and two sons.

3. Notice the book begins with "In the days when Judges ruled there was a famine in the land..." if you're not familiar with what the time of Judges is, it's just one Bible book ahead of this one. It's a tough read, but action-packed!

4. The chapter says that Naomi, her husband Elimelech (may be spelled differently in your translation), and their sons Mahlon and Chilion were Ephrathites. What does that mean? Who were they descendants of?

5. I love reading about how both daughters-in-law wanted to stay with Naomi, so much so that they wept when she sent

them away (verse 9). Why do you think they were so adamant about not leaving her? The book makes no mention of Orpah or Ruth having any children and they were married for 10 years. Why?

6. Ruth, however, didn't just weep. She refused to leave Naomi (verse 16 is my favorite in this chapter!). Honestly, if I were in Ruth's shoes, I would have probably returned home. For that reason I admire Ruth's loyalty.

7. In my efforts not to spoil the end of the book for you (in the event you're not familiar with it), I won't say what happens but I will say that the opening chapter encourages me to trust God's plan for my life. He can see the end from the beginning. Even if it looks like a tragedy right now, it could turn into a beautiful love story that speaks to the power of God's redeeming, delivering, sweet nature.

8. Naomi and Ruth head to Judah, where Naomi is from (verse 19). God is so perfect. They arrive in Bethlehem right at the beginning of the barley harvest, which is significant because remember they're fleeing a famine.

9. It's about to get good y'all! This is just chapter 1.

Prayer focus

Pray that we trust God fully and not lean on our own understanding.

Weekly memory verse

Then the women said to Naomi, "Blessed be the LORD, who has not left you this day without a redeemer, and may his name be renowned in Israel!" Ruth 4:14 (ESV)

Notes

Day 9

Walking in purpose

Waking up to Breakfast with God

Greet Him this morning (Psalm 119:147 tells us why)!

Passage

Ruth 2

Study notes

1. Write your initial reactions to the chapter. Can you see yourself anywhere?

2. My title says "Ruth Meets Boaz." If you've been in church any number of years, you've probably heard of Boaz because he's the man every preacher will tell every woman they should strive to marry. Let's find out why.

3. Here's the scene. Ruth and Naomi are hungry. Naomi knows Boaz through her late husband, Elimelech. Ruth offers to gather leftover food from Boaz's field, hoping to find favor from him. In those days, the poor, sojourners, widows and orphans are allowed to gather food with the permission of the landowner.

4. Boaz notices Ruth working in the field to gather food (verse 5) and inquires about who she is. Remember, she's a Moabite in

Bethlehem so I'm sure no one recognizes her. Then, Boaz shows her extreme kindness (verse 9). What do you think of Boaz's response when Ruth asks why he's being so kind to her (verse 11)? Melts my heart!

5. Naomi refers to Boaz as "one of our redeemers" in verse 20. What does this mean?

6. Boaz's kindness reflects the kindness of God. He showed kindness to a foreigner, went above and beyond to protect and provide for her and was extremely generous toward her when he did not have to be.

7. My thoughts:

    a. Being in God's will (like Naomi and Ruth) is the safest place to be.

    b. When you're doing what you're supposed to be doing (Ruth was working when Boaz noticed her), God will grant you favor; He will take care of you.

    c. Being committed, loyal and kind (as was Ruth) comes with blessing and provision.

    d. Being stretched outside of your comfort zone (as Ruth was in a foreign land) always leads to promotion.

    e. Relationships are so important. Think Naomi and Ruth. What stands out about their relationship?

    f. What else are you thinking? Write it down.

8. Can you see why we love Boaz?!

Prayer focus

That God will supply the people and resources you need in order to fully walk in your purpose.

Weekly memory verse

Then the women said to Naomi, "Blessed be the LORD, who has not left you this day without a redeemer, and may his name be renowned in Israel!" Ruth 4:14 (ESV)

Notes

Day 10

Living a life that reflects the heart of Christ

Waking up to Breakfast with God

Greet Him this morning (Psalm 119:147 tells us why)!

Passage

Ruth 3

Study notes

1. Write your initial reactions to the chapter. Can you see yourself anywhere?

2. There are so many traditional themes in this passage: Ruth washing and anointing herself (making herself attractive and a sign that her mourning was over), the uncovering of Boaz's feet (to signify she wants to marry him), referring to Boaz as a redeemer (male relative who, according to various laws found in the Pentateuch – first 5 books of the Bible, had the privilege or responsibility to act for a relative who was in trouble, danger, or need of vindication).

3. I love when he calls her a "worthy woman" (verse 11). When Boaz met Ruth she was minding her own business, not stagnant, not waiting to be found/redeemed/rescued, rather

she was busy working and he noticed her. What does this teach us about relationships?

4. Boaz recognizes that Ruth can have her choice of husbands (verse 10), but blesses her for choosing him. He refers to it as an "act of kindness." When you're obedient, God blesses your act. Kindness goes a long way—its way made Boaz notice Ruth in chapter 2.

5. Boaz doesn't send Ruth back to Naomi empty-handed. He sends her back with barley. Boaz is a channel of The Lord's recompense and kindness to Naomi. She's been taken care of since she got to Bethlehem. Won't He do it?! How do you perceive Boaz's actions toward Naomi?

6. What does this chapter teach us about godly relationships?

7. In what ways can you show extra kindness today?

8. What is a kinsman redeemer? Hint: It's important and found only in the Book of Ruth.

9. What's required, if anything, in order for a kinsman to redeem?

10. What is a *Goel*? Remember, Googling is not cheating. We're in this to learn and grow.

Prayer focus

That we learn to be kind, committed to the cause of Christ and obedient to His leading in our lives. In essence, that our lives reflect the heart of Christ.

Weekly memory verse

Then the women said to Naomi, "Blessed be the LORD, who has not left you this day without a redeemer, and may his name be renowned in Israel!" Ruth 4:14 (ESV)

Notes

Day 11

Thanking God for redemption

Waking up to Breakfast with God

Greet Him this morning (Psalm 119:147 tells us why)!

Passage

Ruth 4

Study notes

1. Write your initial reactions to Ruth. Can you see yourself anywhere?

2. What a short but glorious book, right? What did you think of Ruth's story? Do you think it's Naomi's story with a lot of Ruth in it?

3. What does the relationship between Boaz and Ruth teach us?

4. What does the relationship between Naomi, Ruth and Boaz show us about God?

5. Naomi is blessed with a new family. Is this a total reversal of the opening of the story?

6. Why do you think God wanted such a short story in the Bible? What does He want us to know through this illustration of how He restored Naomi's life?

7. What have you learned about redemption?

8. Here's where it gets good for me. Y'all ready? Boaz married Ruth and she bares a son names Obed. Here's the importance of that genealogy

    a. Obed is the father of Jesse.

    b. Jesse is the father of David (2 Samuel 7:16 talks about David's forever kingship).

    c. Jesus is the Son of David. Is this title familiar? Jesus is from David's bloodline; his descendant.

9. Ruth marrying Boaz put her in the genealogy of Jesus Christ! This is the same woman who was a childless pagan (worshipper of false gods) at the beginning of the story. Remember, "Your God shall be my God" (chapter 1 verse 16)? If that isn't redemption I don't know what is! Christ's genealogy includes three foreign women: Tamar, Rehad, and Ruth. Look up these women.

10. Does this story carry a theme(s)?

11. Journal what Ruth has taught you.

Prayer focus

Thank God for still redeeming "foreigners" or people who don't have the cleanest history that would qualify them to follow Christ.

Weekly memory verse

Then the women said to Naomi, "Blessed be the LORD, who has not left you this day without a redeemer, and may his name be renowned in Israel!" Ruth 4:14 (ESV)

Notes

Day 12

Review

Waking up to Breakfast with God

Greet Him this morning (Psalm 119:147 tells us why)!

Passage

Spend time in His presence. Review Ruth 1-4.

Study notes

1. Did anything new stick out to you?
2. What can you take away to apply to your life today?
3. What's one commitment, based on the passage, you can make right now?
4. What are you mediating on?

Prayer focus

Pray for revelation while reading. I encourage you to write down your prayers and review them later. Doodle if you'd like.

Weekly memory verse

Then the women said to Naomi, "Blessed be the LORD, who has not left you this day without a redeemer, and may his name be renowned in Israel!" Ruth 4:14 (ESV)

Notes

Day 13

Applying God's Word

Waking up to Breakfast with God

Greet Him this morning (Psalm 119:147 tells us why)!

Study notes

- Spend time in His presence.
- Write freely and have a discussion with Jesus. LISTEN for His voice as you write.
- Turn on worship music -- sometimes I even dance and sing (off key) with Jesus. Song suggestion: "Speak the Name" by Koryn Hawthorne.
- Reflect/Evaluate your own life.
- Have fun!

Applying God's Word

Evaluate your relationships. Consider those that are thriving and those that are expired. How can you be intentional about sustaining Godly relationships, and divorcing toxic ones?

Weekly memory verse

Then the women said to Naomi, "Blessed be the LORD, who has not left you this day without a redeemer, and may his name be renowned in Israel!" Ruth 4:14 (ESV)

Notes

Day 14

Spending time in His presence

Waking up to Breakfast with God

Greet Him this morning (Psalm 119:147 tells us why)!

Study notes

- Think of a current circumstance in your life right now. Remember three things:
    - God sees you.
    - God cares.
    - God has a plan for you.
- Does the story of Ruth speak to that and more?
- How can it aid in your growth? I recommend you jot down your thoughts and ideas.

Prayer focus

Pray for God to redeem those in your life who are not yet believers. Write out their names. Pray for them.

Weekly memory verse

Then the women said to Naomi, "Blessed be the LORD, who has not left you this day without a redeemer, and may his name be renowned in Israel!" Ruth 4:14 (ESV)

Notes

Week 3: Loving others well

Song suggestion: "Just Give Me Jesus" by Unspoken

Good morning!

I want you to know that not only have you been having breakfast with Jesus, but you have also developed your own rhythm for studying God's Word. How incredible that you're seeking Him daily for His guidance! This week we're heading over to 1, 2 and 3 John. Through this journey we are recognizing the difference between reading and studying the Bible (2 Timothy 2:15). God's Word is alive and well. As you read (particularly aloud), it literally breathes over you and restores you. As you study, you expand your arsenal in preparation for life's difficulties. In short, everything you need in life is found between Genesis and Revelation. My sincerest prayer is that we become forever students of God's Word and fall in love with Jesus over and over again, each day for the rest of our lives. First, 2 and 3 John is a great tool to have stored in your heart. Remember, God doesn't do anything just because. Each word breathed into these books matter. And with that, let's eat!

Things to know about 1, 2, 3 John – we'll be studying these books all week so put a bookmark in this page to refer back to.

1. First, 2 and 3 John are written by the apostle John (the same one who wrote the Gospel of John).

2. John was probably written in the vicinity of Ephesus near the end of the first century A.D.

3. The theme is living in the love of God in accordance with the truth of Jesus Christ. This love not only extends to God, but also to other people.

4. John opens 2 John saying "to the elect lady." He's likely referring to a church versus an individual woman.

5. Christian love and compliance with God's commandments are inseparable.

6. False teaching about Christ abounds.

7. Associations and relationships matter – this book explains why.

Day 15

Learning to be still

Waking up to Breakfast with God

Greet Him this morning (Psalm 119:147 tells us why)!

Passage

1 John 1 and 2

Study notes

1. Write your initial reactions. What is the Holy Spirit speaking?
2. Who was John, the author of the Gospel of John and 1, 2, 3 John?
3. What prompted him to write 1 John?
4. Who is his audience?
5. John opens the book speaking in the "we." Who is the "we" he is talking about? Hint: It's not the Father, Son and Holy Spirit as I first thought. Hint 2: Googling is not cheating! Check your sources of course.
6. What are some ways I can perfect the love of God in my life?
7. Am I guilty of loving the world? The desires of the flesh? The desires of the eyes? The pride of life?
8. Repent for number 6.
9. How can I live in this world without loving it?

Prayer focus

Be still. Don't ask God for anything. Sit quietly and think about what you've read. Write down anything that God speaks to you.

Weekly memory verse

"Everyone who goes on ahead and does not abide in the teaching of Christ, does not have God. Whoever abides in the teaching has both the Father and the Son." —2 John 1:9 (ESV)

Notes

Day 16

Uncovering sin and resentment in our hearts

Waking up to Breakfast with God

Greet Him this morning (Psalm 119:147 tells us why)!

Passage

1 John 3 and 4

Study notes

1. Write your initial reactions. Can you see yourself anywhere?
2. What is the difference between sinning and practicing sin? Is there one?

3. What does 1 John 3:8 mean?

4. What is the correlation between love and fear? How does one cancel out the other?

5. After canvassing my life, I realize there are people I don't love the way I'm commanded to. Can you say the same? How can you demonstrate love toward them in action and deed? List the deeds. Plan to do them.

6. Repent for number 4. Ask the Holy Spirit to help.

Prayer focus

Ask God to reveal to you the "hidden" and deep places in your heart where you harbor sin and resentment.

Weekly memory verse

"Everyone who goes on ahead and does not abide in the teaching of Christ, does not have God. Whoever abides in the teaching has both the Father and the Son." –2 John 1:9 (ESV)

Notes

Day 17

Loving others

Waking up to Breakfast with God

Greet Him this morning (Psalm 119:147 tells us why)!

Passage

1 John 5

Study notes

1. Write your initial reactions. What is the Holy Spirit speaking?

2. What does the passage reveal about the testimony of God concerning His Son?

3. Do I possess the confidence found in 1 John 5: 14? How can I strengthen my confidence?

4. What is my approach to sin in the life of my brother and sister?

5. Am I a light to others? How so? How am I not?

6. What is one new thing I learned about eternal life in Heaven?

Prayer focus

Ask God to help you love others the way He loves you.

Weekly memory verse

"Everyone who goes on ahead and does not abide in the teaching of Christ, does not have God. Whoever abides in the teaching has both the Father and the Son." —2 John 1:9 (ESV)

Notes

Day 18

Forgiveness for not loving others the way that He does

Waking up to Breakfast with God

Greet Him this morning (Psalm 119:147 tells us why)!

Passage

2 John

Study notes

1. Write your initial reactions. Can you see yourself anywhere in the text?

2. This is the second time John reminds us to love one another. Why would God place such an emphasis on loving others?

3. Am I doing all I can to show the love of God? How can I improve in this area?

4. What areas of my life are not aligning with God's teaching?

5. Are there any hidden places of hatred and disobedience in my heart that come to mind as I am reading? Ask God to show them.

6. Repent for number 4.

7. Do I know any antichrists? Have I taken part in their "wicked works?"

8. Repent for number 6.

9. What correlation(s) can I draw between truth and love?

Prayer focus

Ask God to forgive you for not loving others like He loves. Make a commitment to turn from your old ways of worshipping your emotions, thoughts, desires and flesh.

Weekly memory verse

"Everyone who goes on ahead and does not abide in the teaching of Christ, does not have God. Whoever abides in the teaching has both the Father and the Son." −2 John 1:9 (ESV)

Notes

Day 19

Showing faith in our actions

Waking up to Breakfast with God

Greet Him this morning (Psalm 119:147 tells us why)!

Passage

3 John

Study notes

1. Write your initial reactions. What is the Holy Spirit speaking?

2. The theme of 3 John is steadfastness in the face of opposition.

3. The recipient of 3 John is Gaius, who is facing trouble during the time of the letter.

4. Walking in truth is so important.

5. The integrity of faith is proven by actions.

6. Church discipline is necessary for a healthy ministry to flourish.

7. The support of traveling Christians is noble and important to God.

8. John rejoices when Gaius, and other Christians, are "walking in

the truth." Do I rejoice when my friends and loved ones succeed, prosper, and obey Christ?

9. Likewise, do I suffer with my friends and loved ones?

10. Pray about numbers 8 and 9.

11. In what ways do I "imitate good?"

12. In what ways do I "imitate evil?"

13. Repent about number 12.

14. Why would God include this short and specific letter in the Bible?

15. Ask the Holy Spirit what He wants you to learn from this passage.

Prayer focus

Pray for faith to be shown in your actions.

Weekly memory verse

"Everyone who goes on ahead and does not abide in the teaching of Christ, does not have God. Whoever abides in the teaching has both the Father and the Son." –2 John 1:9 (ESV)

Notes

Day 20

Praying for revelation

Waking up to Breakfast with God

Greet Him this morning (Psalm 119:147 tells us why)!

Passage

Spend time in His presence. Review 1, 2, 3 John.

Study Notes

1. Did anything new stick out to you?
2. What can you take away to apply to your life today?
3. What's one commitment, based on the passage, you can make right now?
4. What are you meditating on?

Prayer for today

Pray for revelation while reading. I encourage you to write down your prayers and review them later.

Weekly memory verse:

"Everyone who goes on ahead and does not abide in the teaching of Christ, does not have God. Whoever abides in the teaching has both the Father and the Son." —2 John 1:9 (ESV)

Notes

Day 21

Thanking God for everything

Waking up to Breakfast with God

Greet Him this morning (Psalm 119:147 tells us why)!

Study notes

- Spend time in His presence.
- Write freely and have a discussion with Jesus. LISTEN for His voice as you write.
- Turn on worship music – sometimes I even dance and sing (off key) with Jesus. Song suggestion: "Lord You Are My Song" by Charity Gayle.
- Reflect/Evaluate your own life.
- Have fun!

Applying God's Word

Don't ask God for anything. Simply thank Him for everything. Pray for others.

Weekly memory verse

"Everyone who goes on ahead and does not abide in the teaching of Christ, does not have God. Whoever abides in

the teaching has both the Father and the Son." —2 John

1:9 (ESV)

Notes

Week 4: Forgiveness

Song suggestion: "Open Heaven" by Maranda Curtis

Good morning!

Thank you for sticking with your commitment to spend breakfast time with God each day. He's so proud of you! I watched a sermon a few weeks ago by Francis Chan called "What's in Your Closet?" and it inspired me to read Psalm 51. That's where I want to begin this week. For me, this passage is all about forgiveness of oneself. As we read, I want us to examine areas in our lives where we've asked for and received forgiveness, but may still walk in condemnation. Satan is the "accuser of our brethren" (Revelation 12:10). Let's not help him fulfill his job description by constantly choosing to pay for things Jesus already paid for by dying on the Cross. And with that, let's eat!

Things to know about the Psalms – we'll be studying these book all week so put a bookmark in this page to refer back to.

1. The Psalms are a collection of 150 poems covering a variety of topics: love, adoration toward God, sorrow over sin, praises of God, the battle of fear and trust, thankfulness, conflict, a cries for help, devotion to the Word of God, etc.
2. Psalm in Greek is "psalmos" which means "song." The Hebrew name for the book is "Tehillim" which means "praises."

3. David's name appears in at least 73 titles throughout the Book of Psalm, which denotes that he is the most common author. Other authors include the Sons of Korah, Asaph, Solomon and Moses. Some Psalms do not identify an author at all.

4. Most of the Book of Psalm was written in the time of David and Solomon (c. 1010–970 BC).

5. The theme of the book is worship.

6. "Selah", which appears often in the Psalms, indicates a pause, stop or rest.

7. So many gospel songs are actually Psalms that are put to music...which was probably the original intent.

Day 22

Praying from your heart

Waking up to Breakfast with God

Greet Him this morning (Psalm 119:147 tells us why)!

Passage

Psalm 50

Study notes

1. Write your initial reactions. What is the Holy Spirit speaking?

2. This particular Psalm was written by Asaph. He was one of David's worship leaders who authored 12 Psalms. This fact excited me because I thought they were all written by David. It blew my mind, y'all!

3. What were your initial thoughts about the Psalm? Write them down. "Wow" was mine.

4. I often think about sacrifices. Thankfully, since Jesus was the perfect and ultimate sacrifice for our sins, we don't have to go out and grab a bull to sacrifice; however, it is important to make a sacrifice of some sort (time, money, fleshly desires, etc.) unto God. He deserves it and we certainly owe it. Verse 23 talks about a sacrifice of thanksgiving. What are some ways we can glorify God through thanksgiving?

5. Are there different types of sacrifices? The answer is yes. I encourage you to research them.

6. Do you ever feel like you can bribe God? For example, do you say, "I'll give up this for you if you do this for me?" How can we shift our focus from the seeming burden of "doing stuff for God" when we know that He created and owns the order of the universe?

7. I don't know about you but verses 16-22 scared me.

   a. Who is God addressing in this passage?

   b. Take some time to examine your heart.

   c. Do you hate God's discipline (Prov. 3:12)?

   d. Do you say whatever comes to mind (Prov. 18:21)?

   e. Have you forgotten God?

8. If so, repent for number 6.

Prayer focus

Pray from your heart. Focus on sacrifice, forgiveness and on cultivating the true heart of a Christian. You want to be saved for real so that you are not just talking about it, but you are being about it. Put this book down and rush to your knees, bow your head, write your prayer down, cry, or do whatever needs to happen for you to communicate with God through prayer. Afterward, listen expectantly as He communicates back to you. Write down everything He says! Note: it's amazing that the Creator of the universe and Controller of everything in it, desires for you to talk to Him and loves to talk back to you. Don't take prayer for granted.

Weekly memory verse

"Create in me a clean heart, O God, and renew a right spirit within me." – Psalm 51:10 (ESV)

Notes

Day 23

Asking forgiveness

Waking up to Breakfast with God

Greet Him this morning (Psalm 119:147 tells us why)!

Passage

Psalm 51 — I've been waiting for this one. I love this Psalm!

Study notes

1. Write your initial reactions. Can you see yourself anywhere in the text?

2. After David committed adultery with Bathsheba and arranged for her husband to be killed in 2 Samuel 11, the prophet Nathan confronted him. David's conviction prompted the writing of this Psalm. It is so juicy! But before we rush to judge David, let's instead take this opportunity to notice how this Psalm so easily expresses our own sentiments to our sin against God.

3. If you read closely, you notice David appeals to God on the grounds of God's love and mercy. That's where many of us get it wrong. We usually come to God saying, "God I messed up. Please forgive me because I'll never do it again. You know I usually don't do this, but I got caught up..." David took a

different approach. He knew that God is so rich in love, mercy and compassion that if he asked for forgiveness on the account of God's character, he could speak to the very heart and nature of God and be forgiven.

4. Verse 17! When I mess up, I want to be broken like that...in spirit. This is how we get to God's heart and not just His hand. This is how we look on His face and not just His blessings. Let's take a minute to let that sink in.

5. Are you guilty of having this type of attitude after you sin: "I have to be good for a while in order to get back into God's good graces"? David says, "Wash me, and I shall be whiter than snow." He knows that on his best day he is a filthy rag (Isa. 64:6), and he relies on the righteousness of God to cleanse him and restore him. What does this passage teach you thus far about sin and forgiveness?

6. After we sin and ask for forgiveness, we are forgiven according to our belief in Jesus Christ (1 John 1:19 remember?). That means we can walk away rejoicing, whole and free instead of being stuck in guilt and condemnation. God has forgotten about it and therefore we can too. How can we forgive ourselves for something we've asked God to forgive us for?

7. I know this is hard, but we have to let regret and unforgiveness go! God gets no glory out of our wallowing over past sins. That mindset seeks to diminish the work of The Cross.

Prayer focus

Ask God to help you forgive yourself for things you've repented for.

Weekly memory verse

"Create in me a clean heart, O God, and renew a right spirit within me." – Psalm 51:10 (ESV)

Notes

Day 24

Thanking God for His saving power and steadfast love

Waking up to Breakfast with God

Greet Him this morning (Psalm 119:147 tells us why)!

Passage

Psalm 52

Study notes

1. Write your initial reactions. What is the Holy Spirit speaking?

2. To set the scene, this Psalm was written when David was on the run from King Saul who wanted to kill him (1 Sam. 21:1-7). Can you recall a time in your life where you felt like evil was winning? When was the last time you felt as though you couldn't catch a break? Did your enemies seem to prosper while you did not? You're not alone. Jot down how you can use this scripture to combat that mentality.

3. In the midst of literally running for his life, David opens the Psalm by saying "The steadfast love of God endures all the day." That's the confidence we should have no matter the circumstances we face. Take a moment to pray for that level of confidence.

4. Do you see yourself anywhere in verses 1-4? I do.

5. Let's repent together.

6. Righteousness pays off. What are some consequences of evildoing as illustrated in verses 5-7?

7. Compare how you feel about vengeance to what God says in this Psalm about vindicating His people.

Prayer focus

Thank God for His saving, vindicating power and steadfast love.

Weekly memory verse

"Create in me a clean heart, O God, and renew a right spirit within me." – Psalm 51:10 (ESV)

Notes

Day 25

Praying for your enemies

Waking up to Breakfast with God

Greet Him this morning (Psalm 119:147 tells us why)!

Passage

Psalm 53 and Psalm 54

Study notes

1. Write your initial reactions. Can you see yourself anywhere in the text?

2. Fun facts: Psalm 14 and Psalm 53 are similar. The likely purpose of the Psalm is to mourn the fact that mankind does not seek after God and therefore treats one another cruelly.

3. What is God speaking through David in the opening verse of Psalm 53? It packs a punch!

4. Repent here regarding number 3, if necessary. God is looking at us from Heaven right now. What does He see when He looks at you? Will He see one who understands? One who seeks after Him?

5. Repent for number 3. Ask for God's help and believe that you

have it.

6. Psalm 54 describes a time when David's hiding place was compromised by the Ziphites who gave him up to King Saul (1 Sam. 23:19). Just painting the picture.

7. Again, we see that David asks for God's vindication according to God's might. David knows he can do nothing in his own power, and he totally relies on God to save him by His name, not because of who David is. Do you pray like that when you're in trouble? How can you remember to pray to God according to His character and not according to anything you have or haven't done?

8. Who are your enemies? Hint: They are not people. The Bible says that our struggle is not against flesh and blood (Eph. 6:12). Fear, doubt, worry, injustice, demonic spirits, etc. are your enemies. What does Psalm 54:4 say about facing the enemies in your life?

9. If you are here today, it means that God has enabled you to triumph over every challenge you've ever faced. It's not because you're so good, but because He's so good. Keep that in mind the next time trouble arises. How can you show God today that you're thankful for His faithfulness?

10. How can I make more of an effort to trust in the steadfast

love of God? What's one way I can practice trusting God today?

11. Reflect on a time when God vindicated you. Remember, He's the same God. He did it for you back then. He did it for David in Psalm 52. Why do we spend time doubting when God has proven over and over again that He can be trusted?

12. Did you notice the selahs? Just making sure you're paying attention.

Prayer focus

Pray for your enemies (Matt. 5:44).

Weekly memory verse

"Create in me a clean heart, O God, and renew a right spirit within me." – Psalm 51:10 (ESV)

Notes

Day 26

Declaring confidence in God's ability and willingness to answer our prayers

Waking up to Breakfast with God

Greet Him this morning (Psalm 119:147 tells us why)!

Passage

Psalm 55

Study notes

1. Write your initial reactions. What is the Holy Spirit speaking?

2. Can you hear David's earnestness in this Psalm? What parts stood out to you? Write them down.

3. It sounds like David is doing a lot of complaining. Have you ever been there? Today, if you must complain, can you make an effort to take it to God instead of another person? What would that look like?

4. Why do you think David used the dove analogy in verse 6? Remember, nothing in the Bible is by happenstance. Ask the Holy Spirit to draw your attention to the details.

5. Interesting plot twist! Have you ever been betrayed by a

friend? David can relate. Ask God what you can learn through that experience? Have you forgiven that friend?

6. If not, repent for number 4. Forgive them today.

7. Psalm 55:22! Read it aloud a few times. Let it sink in your spirit. The key word here is "righteous." What does "righteous" mean in the context of this passage?

8. The Psalm ends with "But I will trust in you." The end.

9. Write down/think about why you sometimes don't trust God.

10. Write down/think about all the reasons why you should trust God.

Prayer focus

Pray Psalm 51:10.

Weekly memory verse

"Create in me a clean heart, O God, and renew a right spirit within me." – Psalm 51:10 (ESV)

Notes

Day 27

Praying for God's revelation

Waking up to Breakfast with God

Greet Him this morning (Psalm 119:147 tells us why)!

Passage

Spend time in His presence. Review Psalm 50-55.

Study notes

1. Did anything new stick out to you?
2. What can you take away to apply to your life today?
3. What's one commitment, based on the passage, you can make right now?
4. What are you meditating on?

Prayer focus

Pray for revelation while reading. I encourage you to write down your prayers and review them later.

Weekly memory verse

"Create in me a clean heart, O God, and renew a right spirit within me." – Psalm 51:10 (ESV)

Notes

Day 28

Thanking God for everything

Waking up to Breakfast with God

Greet Him this morning (Psalm 119:147 tells us why)!

Study notes

- Spend time in His presence.

- Write freely and have a discussion with Jesus. LISTEN for His voice as you write.

- Turn on worship music – sometimes I even dance and sing (off key) with Jesus. Song suggestion: "Healer" by Isabel Davis.

- Reflect/Evaluate your own life.

Applying God's Word

Write down five takeaways from today's passage. Do you see yourself anywhere in David's current situation? Have you ever found yourself in his state of being? If so, write about it. Think back to how God delivered you. Pray that the Holy Spirit reveal any hidden things in your heart. Put this book down. Repent.

Prayer focus

Pray to desire more of God, for deeper knowledge of Him through His Word, and for the ways in which you can join Him in His work.

Weekly memory verse

"Create in me a clean heart, O God, and renew a right spirit within me." – Psalm 51:10 (ESV)

Notes

Week 5: Keep going

Song suggestion: "Cycles" by Jonathan McReynolds

Good morning!

So much has happened over the past month, wouldn't you agree? The way human beings are set up, we have this thing called free-will. It means that God will not *make* us pay attention to what He's doing in our lives. He will, on the other hand, orchestrate life events to get us to recognize that He is God, and He is jealous of everything we place before Him. I can attest that in this last week. I thank God for BWMK because it has taken me on an adventure of spiritual awakening – a journey that continues to help me prioritize God's presence over anyone and anything. I am starting to question more, research further and seek God deeper than ever before. I pray that it is as much, if not more, of a blessing to you. Thank you for journeying with me.

I will leave you with this word a dear friend spoke into my heart, "bloom where you are planted." I pray that you do the things God is telling you to do right now. Right where you are, I hope that you shine with the light of Jesus and be encouraged that if no one else sees you, God sees you. Trust Him wholeheartedly because, despite what the world looks like right now, He cares for you. "The Lord directs the steps of the godly. He delights in <u>every detail</u> of their lives" Psalm 37:23. Don't stop here. Keep going. Keep studying. And with that, let's eat.

Day 29

Choosing your own adventure part 1

Choose your own adventure using the structure from the last month. Don't know where to start? Ask God to lead you to the passage He desires you study today.

Reminders

1. Write your initial reactions to the passage and any questions you may have. I usually start my journal time with "Dear Jesus" and write whatever is on my mind, including revelations that come to me while reading. If writing isn't your thing and you'd rather talk aloud to God or draw on the blank "Notes" pages, do so.

2. Sit quietly and listen for God to speak to you. Some people hear an audible voice, while others actually think God's words. Whatever you think you hear, write it down. Be open and expectant, asking God to help you discern His voice if you don't know it already.

3. Ask God for an opportunity to live out what you read.

4. Meditate on the Scriptures by focusing your mind on them.

5. Pray.

6. Choose a verse to memorize this week.

Waking up to Breakfast with God

Greet Him this morning (Psalm 119:147 tells us why)!

Passage

_____

Study notes

_____

_____

_____

_____

_____

Prayer focus

_____

_____

Weekly memory verse

_____

_____

Day 30

Choosing your own adventure part 2

Choose your own adventure using the structure from the last month.

Reminders

1. Write your initial reactions to the passage and any questions you may have. I usually start my journal time with "Dear Jesus" and write whatever is on my mind, including revelations that come to me while reading. If writing isn't your thing and you'd rather talk aloud to God or draw on the blank "Notes" pages, do so.

2. Sit quietly and listen for God to speak to you. Some people hear an audible voice, while others actually think God's words. Whatever you think you hear, write it down. Be open and expectant, asking God to help you discern His voice if you don't know it already.

3. Ask God for an opportunity to live out what you read.

4. Meditate on the Scriptures by focusing your mind on them.

5. Pray.

6. Choose a verse to memorize this week.

Waking up to Breakfast with God

Greet Him this morning (Psalm 119:147 tells us why)!

Passage

_____

Study notes

_____

_____

_____

_____

_____

Prayer focus

_____

_____

Weekly memory verse

_____

_____

A special prayer for my sisters

This book began as a series of mini devotional messages posted to Instagram and shared with friends. Although adapted now in this format for a wider audience, I originally dedicated my writing to a community of women studying God's Word together. Here is my prayer for them and for you.

Dear Lord,

I pray for my sister reading this. I pray that You enrich her life with the knowledge of Your Word. I pray that the seeds planted over the last month bloom in her life. I pray that she recognizes You in her daily activities. I pray that You are the most important priority in her life. Thank You for the gift of Your holy Word, which provides us with community, guidance and examples of how to live out Your truths. Give my sister courage to stand on Your Word when she needs strength, security, provision, joy and peace. Allow her to remember that every good and perfect gift comes from You. That nothing else will satisfy her except You. I pray that she relishes in waking up to be with you each day. I pray that her heart is filled with Scriptures that Your Holy Spirit brings to her mind when she needs them. I pray that she is equipped to withstand any trials that arise against her because You have spent time depositing into her. I declare that she is powerful, beautiful and bold for You. I pray that You give her Godly relationships and a community that seeks You above all else. I pray that she dies daily to her flesh, forgives quickly, including herself, and only relies on validation from you to complete her. Be her best friend, Jesus. Sit with her. Love on her. Adorn her with Your Spirit. I pray she never feels alone because You, the Creator of the Universe, desire intimacy with her. She is Your treasure, Your daughter, the one You came to die for. Thank You for loving her well, and for teaching her to love others, including her enemies. Now Lord, I pray that her life is a beacon of hope for others. Separate her so that she never feels the need to assimilate with the world. Cover her with your blood. Thank You for her future, which is bright and full of hope, according to Jeremiah 29:11. Favor her wherever she goes. I pray she lives for Your glory alone. I pray that her life is a worship song to You. I pray Your Scriptures stay on her lips, according to Psalm 119:103. Bless her for her hunger and thirst, after righteousness, according to Matthew 5:6. Thank You for her life. Thank You for everything that has brought her to this moment in time. I pray that she lives in light of eternity henceforth. Thank You for Jesus who saves, rescues and delivers her. She is brand new in You.

In Jesus' name, Amen.

About the Author

Ebonee Rice is a women and girls advocate. Her primary interests are in engaging and connecting women through the transformative power of Jesus Christ. By day, she leads significant early education outreach efforts in Washington D.C. By night, she owns and operates Ebonee Speaks, LLC - a faith-based blog that meets readers at the intersection of Jesus and social justice.

Ebonee believes in leveraging the power of the Gospel and storytelling to bend the arc of the moral universe toward justice. She is committed to amplifying the voices and stories of women in pursuit of equity. She is a two-time alumnae of the University of Southern California's Annenberg School for Communication and Journalism, having earned a B.A. and M.A., and a proud Los Angeles native.

Ebonee lives in Maryland and serves in ministry at iNgage Church in Waldorf. Find her at www.EboneeSpeaks.com and on social media @EboneeSpeaks.

Made in the USA
San Bernardino, CA
08 September 2018